STEP-BY-STEP
FRAME IT
yourself

MATTING & FRAMING

**CREATIVE
PUBLISHING
international**

MINNETONKA, MINNESOTA

Copyright © 1999
Creative Publishing international, Inc.
5900 Green Oak Drive
Minnetonka, Minnesota 55343
1-800-328-3895

President/CEO: David D. Murphy
Vice President/Editorial: Patricia K. Jacobsen
Vice President/Retail Sales & Marketing: Richard M. Miller

Created by: The Editors of
Creative Publishing international, Inc.
Printed on American paper by:
R. R. Donnelley & Sons Co.
10 9 8 7 6 5 4 3

Library of Congress Cataloging-in-Publication Data

Frame it yourself : matting & framing step-by-step.
    p. cm.
  Includes index.
  ISBN 0-86573-419-4 (softcover)
  1. Picture frames and framing. I. Creative Publishing
International.
  N8550.F734 1999
  749'.7--dc21   98-43513

CONTENTS

MATTING & FRAMING

Designing, preparing, and assembling mats and frames allows you to display artwork and memorabilia uniquely. You can achieve professional results and enjoy substantial savings because basic matting and framing methods are easy to master.

Purchase frames to complement your artwork and decorating style at art supply and craft stores. Look for preassembled frames in standard sizes, or look for kits, which allow more customized effects. Discover a greater selection of color, style, and sizing at custom frame shops. Ask custom framers if they have preassembled frames made of excess stock; you may find the perfect frame for less.

Use mats to enhance artwork; a single mat, whether it has a simple bevel-cut opening (page 9), offset corners (page 10), or a nonrectangular opening (page 10), is often all that is needed to highlight a print or photograph. You can also prevent damaging dust and moisture from being trapped against artwork by using a mat. If you want to frame a valuable or sentimental item without a protective mat, use plastic spacers (page 21).

How you choose to mount, or secure, artwork to a mat will vary according to the desired effect. Most artwork is mounted to the back of the mat (page 11), but when you wish to show the outer edges of the paper, it is mounted to a second board behind the mat (pages 12 and 21). Fabric arts may be sewn to or stretched around a mounting board (page 15). Special three-dimensional artwork and memorabilia may be glued or sewn to a mounting board (page 13).

Once you understand the basics of matting and framing, explore the design possiblities of more decorative matting techniques. You may choose to display multiple images (page 26) or to further enhance your artwork by using multiple mats (page 30) or embellished mats (page 38). Or, use multiple mats and raised mats (page 35) when you want to frame a three-dimensional object without the look of a shadow box.

Finally, display your art treasures to their best advantage. Learn how to organize items in effective, balanced groupings. Discover easy tips for hanging framed artwork with other decorative pieces, such as plates and tapestries. See how you can incorporate freestanding frames and accessories with hanging artwork for an attractive presentation.

MATTING & FRAMING BASICS

FRAME SELECTION

Choose a frame style that is correctly proportioned and that complements the artwork, taking into consideration where the picture will be displayed. Be sure the frame can support the weight of the glass and has the correct mounting space for the thickness of the mats and backing.

In many cases, you may be able to use a preassembled, standard-size frame. Unassembled frames, in a variety of styles, are sold in packages containing two sides and are available in 1" (2.5 cm) increments. Sides of different lengths can be combined for a greater variety of sizes. For special displays, you may want to consider ordering a custom frame.

MATTING & FRAMING SUPPLIES

Matting supplies are often available at art supply stores and custom framing shops. Mat boards **(a)** can be found in a wide variety of colors and textures, including silk, marble, linen, and suede. There are two basic types of mat boards: paper and rag. Paper mats, often referred to as acid-free mats, have been buffered to neutralize the acid in the wood pulp; the core, however, is not acid free and will discolor over time. Rag mats, or conservation-quality mats, are the highest grade and do not contain any wood pulp. These mats offer the greatest protection and are recommended for artwork with monetary or sentimental value.

Use a mat cutter **(b)** that cuts a 45° beveled edge. Mat cutters are available in a variety of styles and prices. For best results, select one that has a retractable blade and is marked with a start-and-stop line. Specific cutting instructions may vary with the type of mat cutter. The cutting instructions in this book are for a mat cutter that is pulled toward you. If your mat cutter is designed to be pushed away from you, reverse the cutting instructions.

For accurate measuring, use a metal straightedge **(c)** with ⅟₁₆" (1.5 mm) markings, for cutting mat boards and mounting boards. For best results, choose a straightedge with a rubber or cork backing to prevent slipping, a major cause of cutting inaccuracies. A T-square **(d)** is helpful for ensuring square mats and backing boards.

Use specialty tapes to ensure professional results. Adhesive transfer gum tape **(e),** often called ATG tape, has many applications in framing. This acid-neutral double-stick transfer tape is easy to work with and does not deteriorate with age. This is often the only tape needed for matting and framing inexpensive artwork. Framer's tapes are used for mounting artwork of monetary or sentimental value. These acid-free tapes are available in self-adhesive **(f)** and gummed **(g)** varieties. For the best protection, select an archival-quality tape. Some art supply stores and framing shops will sell framer's tapes in short lengths. Avoid using transparent tape or masking tape; these tapes may lose adhesive quality over time and cause photographs or prints to yellow.

A backing board prevents a print or photograph from warping. Foam-core board **(h)** is a lightweight, acid-neutral backing board. It is available in ⅛" and ³⁄₁₆" (3 and 4.5 mm) thicknesses. Heavyweight ply board is also sometimes used as a backing board. Standard mat board can be used as a backing board in frames measuring 11" × 14" (28 × 35.5 cm) or smaller.

Hardware stores supply and cut single-strength glass **(i),** an inexpensive and distortion-free glass suitable for most artwork. For valuable items, you may want to use a UV-protective glass. Available at framing shops, this glass provides protection from the sun's damaging ultraviolet rays.

BASIC TECHNIQUES

When cutting mats and backing boards, measure the inside mounting space of the frame, and cut the backing and outer mat board ⅛" (3 mm) smaller; also have the glass cut to this dimension. This fitting ease allows for expansion due to humidity. If you are ordering a custom frame, the fitting ease will be allowed when the frame is cut. Order the frame, specifying the exact size of the backing and outer mat board.

For accurate measuring, mark mats using a very sharp, hard lead pencil. To ensure clean beveled cuts, always place a scrap piece of mat under the area to be cut and replace blades frequently.

SINGLE MATS

Single mats can be made in three styles. For a basic single mat (above, right), cut a square or rectangular opening. For additional interest, cut an image opening with offset corners (above). Or, for a unique, nontraditional look, cut an angular, nonrectangular opening (right).

Select a mat board that enhances the colors in the artwork. Usually, a single or outer mat repeats one of the dominant colors in the picture or blends with the colors in the artwork. A mat color that is stronger than the colors of the artwork draws attention away from the artwork.

The width of the mat border on a single mat varies, depending on the size of the artwork and the desired look. As a general rule, make the mat width at least twice the width of the frame molding. For frames 20" × 24" (51 × 61 cm) or larger, cut the mat border at least three times the width of the frame molding. In many cases, all four borders of the mat are equal in width. Contemporary prints, however, often have mats with unequal borders. If desired, the lower border of the mat may be cut wider than the other three to create visual weight.

In order to accurately cut the image opening, start with an accurately cut, squared board. Unless the edges of the artwork will be exposed, such as on artwork with a torn or deckled edge, cut the image opening at least 1/4" (6 mm) smaller than the dimensions of the artwork.

MATERIALS

- Mat board.
- Mat cutter; utility knife.
- Hard-lead, sharp pencil.
- Metal straightedge with rubber or cork backing.
- Metal nail file; artist's burnisher.
- Tracing paper, for angular, nonrectangular opening.

HOW TO CUT A BASIC SINGLE MAT

2 Mark the width of mat borders on wrong side of mat board, measuring from each edge; make two marks on each side. Using a sharp pencil and a straightedge, draw lines connecting the marks.

1 Mark outside dimensions of mat on wrong side of mat board, taking care to mark square corners. Using a utility knife and straightedge, score along marked lines; repeat until board is cut through.

3 Place a scrap of mat board under the area to be cut. Using straightedge, align edge of mat cutter with marked line, placing the start-and-stop line (arrow) of cutter even with upper border line.

4 Push blade into mat. Cut on marked line in one smooth pass; stop when start-and-stop line (arrow) meets lower border line. Pull the blade out of mat. Rotate the board 90°, and cut adjacent side; repeat to cut remaining sides.

5 Remove center piece, or fallout; if a corner is cut short, insert a single-edge razor blade, aligning angle of blade with bevel. Gently slide blade toward corner until fallout is released.

6 Smooth ragged beveled edge, if necessary, using a nail file. On face side of mat, smooth overcuts by lightly rubbing mat with tip of burnisher; this makes overcut less noticeable.

HOW TO CUT A SINGLE MAT WITH OFFSET CORNERS

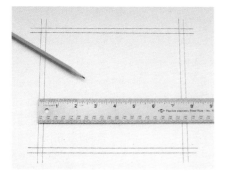

1 Cut and mark the mat board as on page 9, steps 1 and 2. Mark a parallel line ¼" (6 mm) in from each marked line, extending lines beyond image opening.

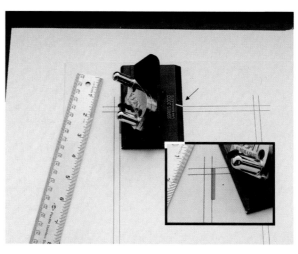

2 Align edge of mat cutter with straightedge, along inside marked line, placing start-and-stop line (arrow) of cutter even with the outer marked line. Push blade into mat. Cut ¼" (6 mm) offset; line can be overcut, extending into the center area of mat. Highlighted line (inset) shows detail of cut. Rotate the board, and repeat at each corner.

3 Reposition the board to cut remaining offset line at each corner; start cut in center area of image opening, and stop when start-and-stop line of cutter is even with outer marked line.

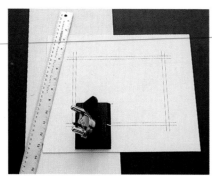

4 Complete the mat as on page 9, steps 3 to 6, aligning the edge of the mat cutter with outer marked lines; align start-and-stop line of the cutter with inner marked lines.

HOW TO CUT A SINGLE MAT WITH AN ANGULAR OPENING

1 Cut the mat as on page 9, step 1. Mark the desired image opening on the tracing paper, using a pencil. Place the paper over artwork, checking for accuracy; re-mark image opening as necessary.

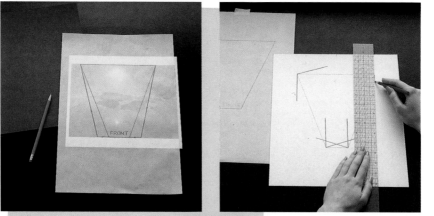

2 Turn the paper over, and position as desired on back of the mat board. Retrace image opening on the marked lines to transfer to mat board. Mark lines at each corner, perpendicular to each side of the image opening, for aligning the mat cutter.

3 Cut the mat as on page 9, steps 3 to 6; align start-and-stop line of the cutter with marked guidelines as shown. Rotate mat as necessary to cut each adjacent line.

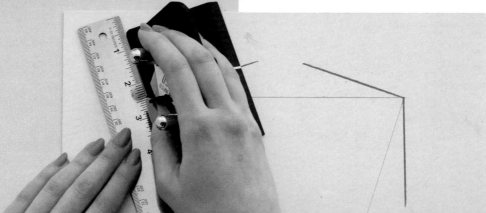

MOUNTING TECHNIQUES

There are a variety of mounting techniques that may be used for securing artwork for framing. When selecting a method, take into consideration the item being mounted, the mat style, and the value of the item being framed.

Hinge mounting is the preferred technique for securing flat pieces of artwork. Depending on the mat style, use one of two methods for hinge mounting. If the image opening of the mat is smaller than the size of the artwork, then the artwork is hinged to the back of the mat board and the backing board is placed behind the picture. If the edges of the artwork are exposed within the image opening of the mat, the picture is hinged to a mounting board. Inexpensive items, such as greeting cards and postcards, can be mounted directly to a mounting board, using double-stick transfer tape.

Artwork may also be dry-mounted at a custom framing shop. This permanent type of mounting is especially recommended for lightweight prints, such as posters, that have a tendency to bubble or ripple.

Most dimensional items can be glued or stitched in place. When using stitches to mount items such as textiles or small pieces of jewelry, choose a thread that matches the item. Or use monofilament fishing line.

Some items, such as coins or dried flowers, can be secured in place using silicone glue or a hot glue gun and glue sticks. Clear silicone glue, available at hardware stores, is the preferred method for valuable or sentimental items. This glue stays flexible and can be removed without damaging the item.

A colored mat board is often used for mounting dimensional items and flat artwork with exposed edges. To prevent the mounting board from warping, especially on large framed artwork, a backing board is recommended.

MATERIALS

- Mat board.
- Utility knife; metal straightedge with rubber or cork backing.
- Backing board, such as foam-core board or heavyweight ply board.
- Mounting board, for hinge mounting to a mounting board and for mounting with glue or hand stitches.
- Framer's tape, for hinge mounting.
- Silicone glue or hot glue gun and glue sticks, for mounting with glue.
- Thread, T-pin, and awl, for mounting with hand stitches.

HOW TO HINGE-MOUNT ARTWORK TO A MAT

1 Cut mat as desired. Place the picture, faceup, on a smooth surface. Cut two strips of framer's tape, each about 1" (2.5 cm) long; secure one-half the length of each strip to back upper edge of artwork as shown.

2 Place the mat, faceup, over artwork, in desired position. Press firmly along upper border of mat to secure the tape. If using gummed framer's tape, moisten the tape before positioning the artwork.

(Continued)

3 Turn mat and artwork over; press firmly to secure the tape. Secure strip of framer's tape to the mat, directly along the edge of the picture and perpendicular to first strip of tape. Repeat at the opposite end.

4 Cut backing board to the same size as the mat. Position artwork and mat on backing board.

HOW TO HINGE-MOUNT ARTWORK TO A MOUNTING BOARD

1 Cut mat as desired. Cut mounting board about 2" (5 cm) larger than mat. Determine placement of artwork; using a pencil, lightly mark position at corners, just inside edges of the artwork.

2 Mark two placement lines for hinges on the mounting board as shown, with length of lines ¼" (6 mm) longer than width of framer's tape. Position lines slightly below the markings for upper edge of the artwork and about 1" to 2" (2.5 to 5 cm) from sides. Mark a third line, centered below markings for upper edge, as shown. Using a utility knife and a straightedge, cut a slit at each marking.

3 Cut three strips of framer's tape about 1½" (3.8 cm) in length. Working from front side of mounting board, insert a strip of tape through each slit, adhesive side up, allowing about ½" (1.3 cm) of tape to extend on front side of board. Secure tape to back side of mounting board.

4 Place artwork, faceup, over front side of mounting board, aligning corners with markings. Press firmly to secure artwork to tape. If using gummed tape, moisten tape before positioning artwork.

5 Place mat over mounting board, with artwork positioned correctly in the opening of mat; mark along the outer edges of mat, using pencil. Cut the mounting board on marked lines. Cut backing board to same size as mounting board.

HOW TO MOUNT ITEMS USING GLUE

2 Apply a bead of clear silicone glue or hot glue to back of item; place item over mounting board, aligning edges of item with markings. Allow the silicone glue to cure for 24 hours, or hot glue to cool completely. Complete as in step 5, opposite.

1 Cut mat as desired. Cut mounting board about 2" (5 cm) larger than mat. Determine placement of item; using a pencil, lightly mark position at corners, just inside edges of item.

HOW TO MOUNT ITEMS USING HAND STITCHES

1 Cut mat as desired. Cut the mounting board about 2" (5 cm) larger than the mat board. Position the item over mounting board as desired. Determine locations where the item can be supported with small stitches; use a T-pin to mark the mounting board by puncturing it.

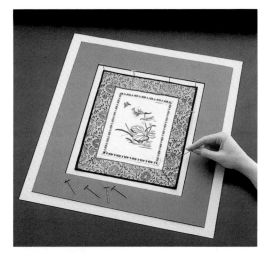

2 Remove item. Puncture holes at markings and, again, ⅛" (3 mm) from each marking, using awl.

3 Reposition item. Using thread that matches item, secure it to mounting board at each set of holes, taking about two stitches. From the back of board, tie thread tails, and secure them to board with tape. (Contrasting thread was used to show detail.)

4 Lift mounting board, and check for proper support of item; take additional stitches, if necessary. Complete as in step 5, opposite.

FRAMING NEEDLE ARTS

Needle art, including cross-stitch, crewelwork, drawnwork, and needlepoint, adds a warm, personal touch to wall displays. Framing and matting draw attention to the piece and offer protection.

In order to display needle art without any wrinkles or bubbles, stretch fabric or canvas artwork around a foam-core mounting board. When mounting needlepoint, which requires firmer stretching, reinforce the foam-core board with a piece of mat board.

Needle-art pieces worked on fabric can be secured to the mounting board using double-stick transfer tape or sequin pins. The tape method is quick and easy; however, the tape may discolor the fabric over time. For needle-art pieces of value, sequin pins are recommended; the pins can be removed if you decide you want to use the piece for another project at a later date. Because of the firmer stretching required for needlepoint projects, the canvas is stapled to the mounting board.

For easy mounting, allow several inches of fabric or canvas on each side of the design. If necessary, fabric strips can be stitched to the sides of the needle-art design. Be sure the needle art is clean before stretching it. Needlepoint pieces may need to be blocked before framing. Clip any loose threads on the back side, since loose thread tails may create streaks on the finished piece.

In order to accurately position the needle-art design in the image opening of the mat, the mounting board is cut smaller than the frame opening. This allows you to adjust the position of the mounting board, if the needle art is not accurately centered.

A single mat is often all that is needed to raise the glass above the surface of the stitching. If additional space is needed between the glass and the stitching, cut a multiple mat (page 30) or raised mat (page 35). For the best protection of all needle-art projects, use acid-free foam-core boards and mat boards.

MATERIALS

- $\frac{3}{16}$" (4.5 mm) foam-core board.
- Mat board and packing tape, for stretching needlepoint.
- Stainless steel T-pins.
- Double-stick transfer tape or ATG tape; framer's tape.
- Sequin pins, for stretching needle art worked on fabric, optional.
- Heavy-duty stapler and $\frac{3}{16}$" (4.5 mm) staples, for stretching needlepoint.
- Utility knife and straightedge.
- Firmly woven fabric, if necessary to increase size of needle art.

HOW TO STRETCH NEEDLE ART WORKED ON FABRIC

1 **Double-stick transfer tape.** Cut foam-core board at least 2" (5 cm) larger than the image opening of mat.

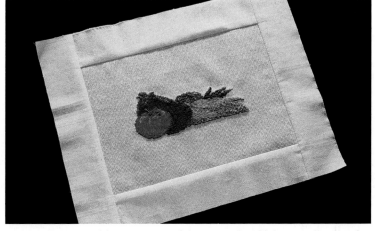

2 Stitch strips of firmly woven fabric to sides of the needle art, if necessary to increase size; allow at least 1" (2.5 cm) on each side for wrapping and stretching fabric around board.

(Continued)

15

3 Center the needle art, right side up, over foam-core board. Insert a T-pin, through fabric and into the edge of foam-core, at center of one side. Aligning grain of fabric with edge of board, pin fabric at each corner of same side, pulling the fabric taut between pins. Repeat to stretch and pin fabric to adjacent side, then remaining sides.

4 Stretch and pin the fabric between the T-pins, completing one side at a time and spacing T-pins about every ½" (1.3 cm).

5 Recheck that design is straight; repin as necessary. Check that the fabric is taut by smoothing finger across piece; you should not be able to push any excess fabric. Repin fabric as necessary.

6 Secure double-stick transfer tape to back of board, close to the edges; apply second layer of tape over the previous layer. Wrap excess fabric to back of board, pulling firmly and securing to tape; complete one side at a time, starting in the center and working toward corners.

7 Remove T-pins. Fold fabric at the corners, trimming any excess; secure with tape. Secure needle art to mat board (opposite).

Sequin pins.
Follow pages 15 and 16, steps 1 to 5. Insert sequin pins into edges of the board, at ¼" (6 mm) intervals, removing T-pins. Fold in the excess fabric at corners; secure with hand stitching. Secure needle art to mat board (opposite).

HOW TO STRETCH NEEDLEPOINT

1 Cut the foam-core board 1" to 2" (2.5 to 5 cm) larger than the image opening of the mat. Cut a piece of mat board the same size as the foam-core board; secure to the foam-core board, using double-stick transfer tape. Mat board side is the back of the mounting board.

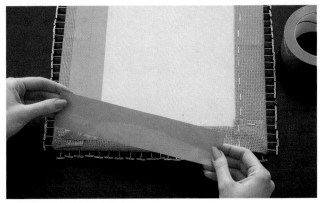

2 Stretch and secure needlepoint following steps 3 to 5 opposite. Wrap the excess canvas to back side of the board, pulling firmly, and staple. Complete one side at a time, starting in center and working toward corners. Fold in excess canvas at corners; staple.

3 Secure raw edges of canvas to back of the board, using packing tape. Remove T-pins. Secure needle art to mat board (below).

HOW TO SECURE STRETCHED NEEDLE ART TO A MAT BOARD

1 Position mat over needle art, centering design. Holding needle art and mat firmly, turn piece over; tape needle art to mat board, using framer's tape.

2 Cut pieces of foam-core board to fill the areas between needle art and edge of the mat board; secure each piece to the mat, using double-stick transfer tape. Cut the backing board to same size as the top mat. Assemble the picture (page 18).

PICTURE & FRAME ASSEMBLY

Picture assembly, called fitting, secures the artwork, mats, glass, and backing or mounting board in the frame. A paper backing, called a dust cover, prevents dust and insects from working their way to the front of the artwork. Rubber bumpers, attached to the lower corners of the frame, allow air to circulate behind the picture and protect the wall.

If necessary, the assembled picture can extend beyond the mounting depth of the frame. Specialty offset hardware is available in several depths to accommodate this type of frame assembly. In general, the boards should not extend more than 1/4" (6 mm) beyond the mounting depth of the frame.

When framing valuable artwork, apply an acrylic clear finish to the unfinished wood at the back of the frame before assembling. This sealer protects the artwork from the acids in the wood frame.

For metal sectional frames, follow the manufacturer's directions for assembling and fitting the frame; this style frame generally comes with complete assembly instructions.

Picture-assembly materials and tools, from top to bottom, include a framer's fitting tool, brown craft paper, foam-core board, artwork, mat, glass, awl, picture wire, rubber bumpers, double-stick transfer tape, frame, screw eyes, brads, and offset hardware.

HOW TO ASSEMBLE A PICTURE & WOODEN FRAME

MATERIALS

- Wooden picture frame.
- ¾" (2 cm) brads, for attaching frame; or offset hardware and screws.
- Framer's fitting tool or slip-joint pliers, for assembly with brads.
- Brown craft paper and double-stick transfer tape, or ATG tape, for assembly with brads.
- Two screw eyes.
- Self-adhesive rubber bumpers.
- Small awl; picture wire.
- Pressure-sensitive frame-sealing tape, for assembly with offset hardware.

1 **Assembly with brads.** Cut mat as desired. Mount artwork (pages 11 to 13). Clean both sides of glass thoroughly, using glass cleaner and lint-free cloth. Position glass over picture and mounting board, with edges even; do not slide glass over surface of the mat. Position frame over glass. Check glass for lint or dust. Slide fingers under backing board, and turn frame over.

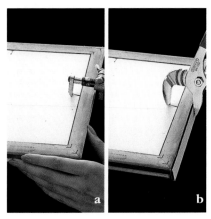

2 Insert ¾" (2 cm) brads into the middle of each side of the frame, using framer's fitting tool **(a)**. Or use slip-joint pliers **(b)**, protecting the outside edge of the frame with strip of cardboard.

3 Insert brads along each side, 1" (2.5 cm) from the corners and at about 2" (5 cm) intervals.

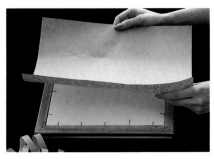

4 Attach double-stick transfer tape to back of the frame, about ⅛" (3 mm) from outside edges. Cut brown craft paper 2" (5 cm) larger than the frame; place paper on back of frame, securing it to center of each edge of frame and stretching the paper taut.

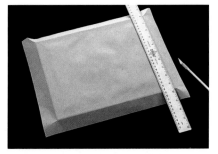

5 Working from center out to each corner, stretch paper and secure to frame. Crease paper over outside edge of frame. Using a straightedge and utility knife, trim the paper about ⅛" (3 mm) inside the creased line.

6 Mark placement for the screw eyes, using an awl, about one-third down from the upper edge; secure screw eyes into the frame. Thread wire two or three times through one screw eye; twist the end. Repeat at opposite side, allowing slack; wire is usually about 2" to 3" (5 to 7.5 cm) from top of the frame when hung. Secure rubber bumpers to back of frame, at lower corners.

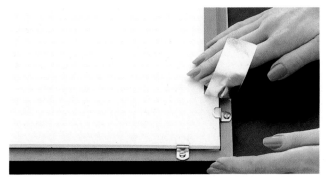

Assembly with offset hardware. Assemble artwork and frame as in step 1, above; secure in place with offset hardware, spacing hardware about 1½" (3.8 cm) from each corner and at about 6" to 8" (15 to 20.5 cm) intervals; predrill screw holes in hardwood frames. Apply frame-sealing tape to edges of frame to seal assembly. Complete assembly as in step 6.

DISPLAYING OLD PHOTOGRAPHS & DOCUMENTS

Old photographs and documents are often cherished for their historic or sentimental appeal. Today, there is increasing interest in preserving and displaying family photographs and documents that give an account of one's ancestral history, as well as in collecting vintage postcards, artwork, and news clippings.

Photographs and documents can be matted and framed for a traditional look. Or they can simply be attached to a mounting board and then framed without a mat; this is sometimes referred to as top mounting. To make sure that cherished items can be handed down from generation to generation, frame the items using the techniques for conservation framing. With conservation framing, the materials and procedures used help protect photographs and documents from atmospheric acidity and sunlight and allow for expansion during periods of high humidity.

While true conservation framing, or museum mounting, requires specialty materials and the skills of an expert, there are many precautions you can take when framing items yourself.

To protect photographs and documents from acids that cause yellowing and disintegration, use acid-free mat boards and mounting boards. Although regular mat and mounting boards are buffered to neutralize the acid in the wood pulp, purchase conservation-quality boards made from 100 percent cotton rag for maximum protection. To seal the acids that are in the wooden frame, apply a clear acrylic finish to the raw wood of the frame. To best preserve the framed item, use UV-protective glass. This glass is more expensive than standard glass, but provides protection from 95 percent of the sun's damaging ultraviolet rays.

To avoid trapping moisture against the photograph or the document, it is important to allow air space under the glass. When you are not matting the photograph, use spacers to keep the glass from touching it. Narrow plastic strips, designed with a channel that fits over the edge of the glass, are available from framing stores. The spacers can be cut to the length of the glass.

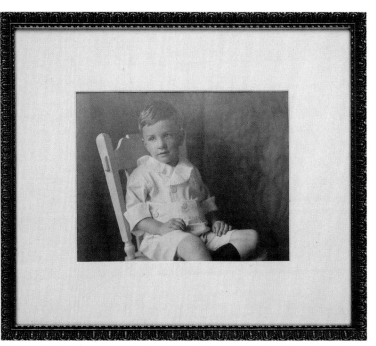

Cherished photograph (above) is hinge-mounted with a bevel-cut mat. Opposite, a document over 100 years old is hinge-mounted without a mat, which allows the torn edges to show.

Gummed linen framer's tape is the preferred tape for mounting, because it is acid free. Acid-neutral double-stick transfer tape, or adhesive transfer gum (ATG) tape, may be used to attach the paper dustcover to the back of the frame.

Mats are easy to cut using a mat cutter with a 45° beveled edge. Mat cutters come in a variety of styles and prices. For best results, select one that has a retractable blade and is marked with a start-and-stop line. This line acts as a guide, making it easier to cut perfect corners. Specific cutting instructions may vary with the type of mat cutter.

HOW TO HINGE-MOUNT A PHOTOGRAPH
OR DOCUMENT WITHOUT A MAT

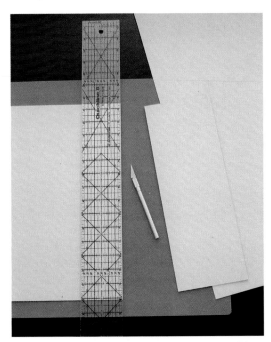

2 Fold 1¼" (3.2 cm) strip of linen framer's tape, gummed side out, folding back ¼" to ½" (6 mm to 1.3 cm), depending on the size and weight of the document or photograph. Place document facedown on smooth, clean surface. Moisten short side of strip and secure to document as shown, positioned near one end, with the folded edge of the strip a scant ⅛" (3 mm) below upper edge of document. Repeat at opposite end.

1 Determine size to cut the mounting board by subtracting ⅛" (3 mm) from the dimensions of frame opening; mark wrong side of mounting board, making sure corners are square. Using a utility knife and straightedge, score along marked line; repeat until board is cut through.

3 Moisten the remainder of strip; secure to mounting board, positioning the document as desired.

HOW TO ASSEMBLE A PHOTOGRAPH
OR DOCUMENT IN A WOODEN FRAME

MATERIALS

- Wooden picture frame and glass; clear acrylic finish, for sealing raw wood of frame.
- Plastic spacers with channels for glass, for assembling a picture without a mat.
- ¾" (2 cm) brads, for attaching frame.
- Framer's fitting tool or slip-joint pliers.

- Brown craft paper, for backing paper.
- Double-stick transfer tape, or ATG tape.
- Two small screw eyes.
- Self-adhesive rubber bumpers.
- Small awl; braided picture wire; masking tape.

1 Seal raw wood of the frame, using clear acrylic finish; allow to dry. Bevel-cut a mat (page 9), if desired. Hinge-mount document or photograph (pages 11 and 12).

2 Clean both sides of glass thoroughly, using glass cleaner and lint-free cloth. If frame is being assembled without a mat, cut plastic spacers to fit on each side of glass. Attach narrow channels of spacers to sides of glass, or, if using thick glass, attach wider channels; spacers should fit snugly. Complete as on page 19, steps 1 to 6.

FRAMED MIRRORS

Create a focal point in the room by using a beautiful picture frame as the frame for a wall mirror. A smaller picture frame can be used as a tabletop mirror, to display perfume bottles or a grouping of votive candles.

Be sure the *rabbet,* the recess on the inner edge of the picture frame, can accommodate a ⅛" or ¼" (3 or 6 mm) mirror plus a ⅛" or ¼" (3 or 6 mm) hardboard backing. Keep in mind that ⅛" (3 mm) mirrors weigh 1½ lb. (750 g) per sq. ft. (0.32 sq. m) and ¼" (6 mm) mirrors weigh 3¼ lb. (1.6 kg) per sq. ft. (0.32 sq. m); the ⅛" (3 mm) thickness works well without causing distortion in the mirrored image, except in very large mirrors. Custom-size mirrors are available from glass companies and specialty mirror stores. Have the mirror cut to the length and width that fits within the rabbet.

After placing the mirror and the hardboard backing into the rabbet, hold the mirror in place by nailing brads into the frame as if mounting a picture. To hang the framed mirror on the wall, secure two swivel hangers onto the back of the frame. Then hook the swivel hangers onto picture hangers or mirror hangers, mounted on the wall. Select picture hangers or mirror hangers that will support the weight of the mirror; weight limitations are specified on the package.

Picture frames may be used to frame wall or tray mirrors, for a custom look and size. The vanity tray above uses a picture frame embellished with beads.

HOW TO MOUNT A FRAMED MIRROR

MATERIALS

- Picture frame.
- Mirror, cut to fit within rabbet of picture frame; thickness of mirror may be ⅛" or ¼" (3 or 6 mm), depending on depth of rabbet.
- ⅛" or ¼" (3 or 6 mm) hardboard, for backing.
- Corner braces and screws, to strengthen mitered corners of mirror; screws must be shorter than thickness of mirror frame, to prevent puncturing front of frame.
- Double-stick framer's tape and brown craft paper, for dust cover on the back of the mirror frame.
- ¾" (2 cm) brads; framer's fitting tool or split-joint pliers.
- Two swivel hangers and screws, to mount onto the back of the mirror frame.
- Two picture hangers or mirror hangers and screws, to mount onto wall; select hangers that will support the weight of the mirror.
- Jigsaw; awl; mat knife.

1 Place the picture frame facedown. Secure corner braces across mitered corners of the frame, using an awl to puncture pilot holes for screws into frame as shown; then screw braces to the frame.

2 Cut backing board from hardboard to same size as the mirror; wipe clean. Set the mirror facedown into rabbet of the picture frame; then place hardboard over mirror, within rabbet.

3 Insert ¾" (2 cm) brads into the middle of each side of frame, using a framer's fitting tool **(a).** Or use split-joint pliers **(b),** protecting the outer edge of the molding with a strip of cardboard.

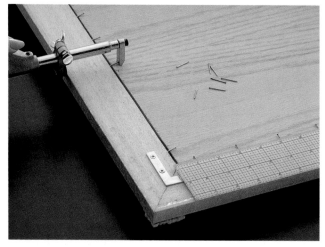

4 Insert brads along each side, about 1" (2.5 cm) from the corners and at 2" (5 cm) intervals.

5 Attach double-stick framer's tape to back of frame, about ⅛" (3 mm) from outer edges. Remove paper covering.

6 Cut brown craft paper 2" (5 cm) larger than frame. Place paper on the back of the frame; stretch paper taut at center of each side, creasing it over outer edge of frame and securing it to tape.

7 Stretch paper and secure it to the tape, working from the center out to each corner; crease paper over outer edge of frame.

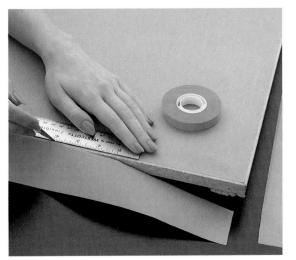

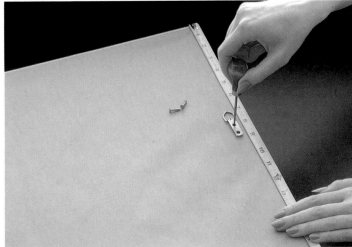

8 Trim the paper about ⅛" (3 mm) inside the creased line, using mat knife.

9 Mark the placement for swivel hangers on sides of frame, about one-third of the way down from the top. Centerpunch frame with an awl, and attach swivel hangers with screws.

10 Measure and mark placement for mirror or picture hangers on wall, so hangers will be spaced same distance apart as swivel hangers on frame; use a carpenter's level to evenly mark lines horizontally. Secure mirror or picture hangers at the markings. Hang the mirror.

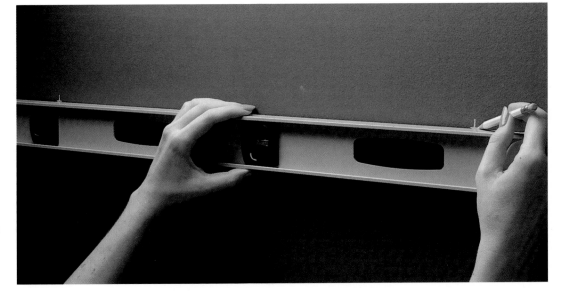

MATS WITH
MULTIPLE OPENINGS

The Olson Reunion

Display related items in a single mat and frame, using a mat with multiple openings. These mats are perfect for showcasing time-lapse pictures and family photos. Or use a mat with multiple openings to create a space for titling or dating a photograph or piece of artwork.

When cutting mats with multiple openings, treat each opening as a separate, single mat. Completing one opening before starting another ensures that the bevel cuts are at the correct angle.

Because of the precise measurements required, mats with multiple openings are best suited for single mats. It is difficult to cut double or triple mats with multiple openings that align accurately.

Experiment with the positioning of the artwork in order to find a pleasing arrangement. In general, the width of the outer mat border should be the same on all four sides. The width of the mat board between the images is usually narrower than the width of the outer mat border. This helps the images relate to each other and focuses attention inward.

MATERIALS

- Mat board.
- Basic mat-cutting materials (page 9).
- Art eraser.

HOW TO CUT A MAT WITH MULTIPLE OPENINGS

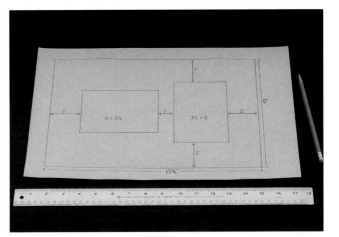

1 Arrange artwork as desired on sheet of paper; determine dimensions of image openings and borders, including outer border. Mark borders and image openings on paper.

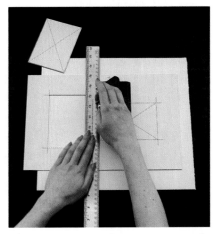

2 Transfer markings to back side of paper, if arrangement is not symmetrical. Label for back of mat; use this paper as a guide for marking back of mat board.

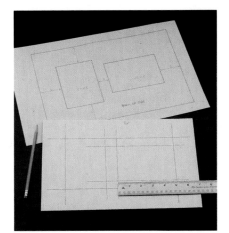

3 Cut mat and mark outer border as on page 9, steps 1 and 2. Transfer the markings for image openings, from paper guide to back of the mat board, extending the marked lines beyond the dimensions of the image openings. Remeasure each opening for accuracy.

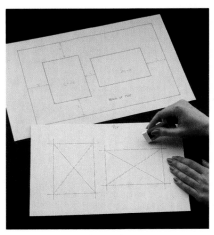

4 Mark an X through each image opening. Erase all but ½" (1.3 cm) of lines that are not to be cut, to use as guide for aligning straightedge.

5 Cut image openings as on page 9, steps 3 to 6; complete one opening before starting another.

MORE IDEAS FOR MULTIPLE OPENINGS

Series of rectangular openings creatively highlights artwork.

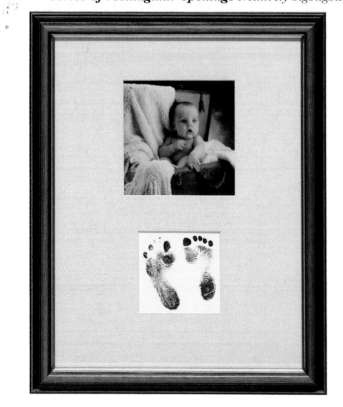

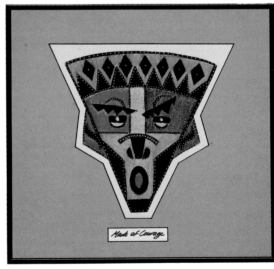

Title opening (above) is used to identify a piece of artwork. The angular opening (page 10) follows the contours of the artwork.

Double openings (left) display a baby picture and infant footprints.

Triple openings (opposite) showcase a collection of photos.

MULTIPLE MATS

Multiple mats consist of two or more layered mats that have successively larger image openings. These mats provide the opportunity to use several mat colors when framing a single piece of artwork. Multiple mats lead the eye into the image and add depth and richness; the more mats used, the stronger the effect.

Framing shops have mat corner samples available to help you select mat colors. Experiment with different combinations, noticing the features of the artwork that are highlighted with each combination.

A standard width for undermats is ¼" (6 mm); however, this measurement often ranges from ⅛" (3 mm) to ½" (1.3 cm), depending on the look you desire. Different widths can be used in any combination, for a variety of effects. Experiment by layering mat boards in various combinations, exposing different widths for the inner mats to find the arrangement you like best. Keep in mind that light-colored mats will appear wider than dark-colored mats.

When cutting multiple mats, cut the outer, or top, mat first. Then secure the next mat to the back of the completed mat, and cut. Repeat this process for each additional mat.

Precise measuring and cutting are critical when cutting multiple mats. Recheck your calculations to avoid mistakes. Discrepancies of as little as ¹⁄₁₆" (1.5 mm) may be noticeable. For easier reference when cutting, it may be helpful to mark the desired widths for each mat, using a different-colored pencil for each mat.

MATERIALS

• Mat board.

• Basic mat-cutting materials (page 9).

• Double-stick transfer tape, or ATG tape.

1 Cut top, or outer, mat board to the outside dimensions as on page 9, step 1. Determine the size of image opening and width of mat borders for bottom, or inner, mat. Mark width of mat borders for bottom mat on top mat, as on page 9, step 2; extend marked lines to edges of mat board.

2 Determine the width of exposed portion of mat border for inner, or first, mat. Mark this measurement on top mat, measuring from previously marked lines toward outside edges of board; extend marked lines to the edges of mat board.

3 Determine the width of exposed portion of second mat. Mark this measurement on top mat as in step 2. Repeat for any additional mats.

4 Cut the image opening in top mat, on outer marked lines as on page 9, steps 3 to 6. Reposition fallout section from top mat for support when cutting. Apply double-stick transfer tape to back side of outer mat along inside edges; apply a short strip of tape to center fallout section.

5 Cut the outside dimensions of mat board for the next mat and any remaining mats ½" (1.3 cm) smaller than top mat. Center next mat facedown, over back side of top mat; press in place.

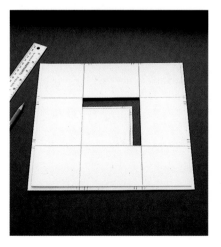

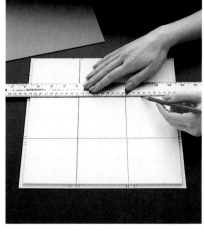

6 Mark width of border for the next mat, using the next set of markings around the edges of the top mat as a guide. Cut mat. Reposition the fallout section and continue as in step 7 if cutting additional mats.

7 Apply double-stick transfer tape to back side of the mat along inside edges and center fallout section. Center next mat facedown over back side of mat; press in place. Continue as in step 6.

MORE IDEAS FOR MULTIPLE MATS

Triple mat with offset corners (below) gives a distinctive look to an old document.

Six mats (bottom, left) in vibrant colors add significance to a child's drawing.

Quadruple mat (left) draws out colors in the artwork. The mats are cut in a variety of widths for more interest.

Seven mats (left) create a mounting depth suitable for framing a dimensional fossil.

Three monochromatic mats (above) add richness to a simple display of pressed leaves.

RAISED MATS

Create a shadow-box effect for artwork by raising mats above the surface of the mounting board. This technique is used to frame dimensional items, such as handmade paper, jewelry, shells, and coins. Raised mats can also be used with flat artwork to add dimension.

The mats are raised by securing spacer strips of foam-core board, cut slightly narrower than the width of the mat border, to all four sides of the mat. This technique can be applied to all mat styles.

For a basic raised mat, secure spacer strips to the back of a single mat. Spacer strips may be stacked to a depth of about ⅝" (1.5 cm). Layers thicker than this may be visible when the picture is viewed from an angle. This style mat is suitable for framing dimensional objects up to about ½" (1.3 cm) in depth.

For added dimension, separate multiple mats for a stacked-and-layered effect. This technique is quite dramatic and allows deeper framing depths, without the possibility of the foam-core board showing.

Foam-core boards are available in ⅛" and 3/16" (3 and 4.5 mm) thicknesses. Choose the board or combination of boards that will give the desired depth for the object you are framing. The glass should not touch the object being framed. If you are stacking foam-core spacers, be sure the mounting depth of the frame can accommodate the thickness of all the layers. It may be necessary to select a shadow-box frame.

Complete all mat cutting and apply any embellishments to the mat (page 38) before securing the spacer strips.

MATERIALS

- Mat board.
- Basic mat-cutting materials (page 9).
- Foam-core board.
- Double-stick transfer tape, or ATG tape.

Triple mat (above) is raised between successive mats, adding interest to an architectural print. Single raised mat (opposite) provides the mounting depth needed for displaying a collection of buttons.

HOW TO MAKE A RAISED SINGLE MAT

 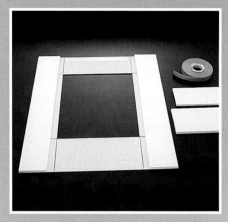 

1 Cut single mat (page 9). Mark the dimensions of the spacer strips for sides of mat on foam-core board, with length of strips equal to length of mat sides and width of strips ½" (1.3 cm) narrower than mat border width. Score repeatedly on the marked lines, using a utility knife and straightedge, until the foam-core board is cut through.

2 Cut strips of double-stick transfer tape; secure them to back of the mat board near the outer edges. Position the foam-core strips on sides of mat board, aligning outer edges; press to secure.

3 Cut and apply second layer of spacer strips, if desired, cutting strips ¼" to ½" (6 mm to 1.3 cm) narrower than the previous strips. Repeat, if desired, for third layer.

MORE IDEAS FOR RAISED MATS

Raised single mat *gives dimension to pressed leaves and handmade paper.*

Raised mat with window-pane opening *gives the effect of looking out through a window. Inner panels are supported with narrow strips of foam-core board.*

HOW TO MAKE A RAISED MULTIPLE MAT

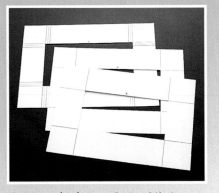

1 Cut multiple mat (page 31); in step 4, use short strips of double-stick transfer tape positioned toward outer edges of the mat. Gently separate mats; center and mark an X along inner opening of same side of each mat to use as guides for realignment.

2 Cut and secure spacer strips to back of top mat, following steps 1 and 2, opposite. Secure strips of double-stick transfer tape to back of spacer strips.

3 Center top mat faceup, over face side of inner mat, aligning marked sides; press in place. Repeat for each successive mat.

Raised mat with multiple openings displays flat artwork and dimensional floral materials.

Mount flat artwork (page 11), and support with separate backing board. Secure backing board to mat board, using double-stick transfer tape; then apply foam-core spacer strips to mat as in steps 1 and 2, opposite.

EMBELLISHED MATS

Mats can be embellished using ink lines, strips of graphic tape or marbleized paper, and decorative rub-on transfers. Each method has its own distinctive style. The methods can also be combined for additional interest.

Embellished mats are usually used when a traditional look is desired; however, contemporary effects can also be achieved.

Decorating mats with ink lines, often referred to as French lines, was originally done using French line pens and inkwells. The same effects are easily achieved using permanent, fine-point markers.

Pressure-sensitive tape gives the effect of French lines with a slightly bolder look. This tape is available in several widths and colors at stationery and office supply stores.

French lines are generally marked close to the inner edge of the mat to draw the eye inward. Multiple lines are usually spaced no more than ½" (1.3 cm) apart. In general, use light-colored lines near the inner edge of the mat and dark lines near the outer edge.

For a more vibrant accent, apply narrow strips of marbleized paper around the image opening. These strips are usually applied as single bands, generally ranging in width from ⅛" to ⅜" (3 mm to 1 cm). Bands wider than this detract from the artwork. Framing shops supply self-adhesive pieces of marbleized paper in a variety of colors. Or make your own strips, using marbleized paper and double-stick transfer tape. When selecting papers, choose one with a dominant color that is repeated in the artwork.

Rub-on transfers, designed especially for embellishing mats, are available in a variety of designs, including flourishes, lines, and letters. For best results, keep the applications simple. One or two flourishes are usually all that is needed.

Choose smooth-surfaced mats and complete all cutting before applying embellishments. These techniques are not suitable for heavily textured or fabric mats. Avoid metallic mats when using ink lines. You may want to test the technique first on a scrap piece of the mat board. When applying multiple rows, start at the inner edges of the mat and work toward the outer edges.

HOW TO EMBELLISH A MAT
USING INK LINES

MATERIALS

- Mat.
- Permanent, fine-point markers.
- Metal straightedge.
- Art eraser.

1 Mark placement of lines on right side of mat, with short marks at outer edges of mat. Mark start and stop of each line with a light pencil line ¼" to ½" (6 mm to 1.3 cm) long.

2 Align a straightedge so the markings are just visible. Holding marker in an upright position, mark line on one side of the mat, using one continuous motion; start and stop the line just inside markings. Lift marker.

(Continued)

3 Turn mat 180° to opposite side; align straightedge, and mark the line. Allow ink lines to dry; then mark lines on remaining sides. Repeat to draw any additional lines. Allow ink to dry.

4 Erase pencil marks, using an art eraser and a light, circular motion.

HOW TO EMBELLISH A MAT USING PRESSURE-SENSITIVE TAPE

MATERIALS

- Mat.
- Pressure-sensitive tape.
- Metal straightedge.
- Mat knife.
- Artist's burnisher; tracing paper.
- Art eraser.

1 Follow page 39, step 1. Cut tape about 2" (5 cm) longer than needed. Holding tape taut, align with marked line; lightly smooth in place, leaving excess tape at ends loose. Repeat on opposite side.

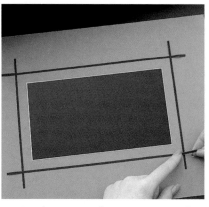

2 Apply tape to the remaining sides, overlapping ends at corners.

3 Position straightedge diagonally over corner of mat at 45° angle to tape. Using mat knife, cut through the upper strip of tape. Remove the trimmed end.

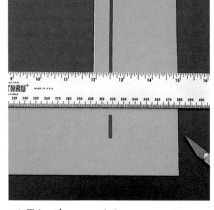

4 Trim the remaining excess tape even with outer edge of tape on adjacent side, using straightedge and mat knife.

5 Repeat steps 3 and 4 at remaining corners. Place tracing paper over tape; rub gently, using burnisher and taking care not to mar mat. Erase any pencil marks, using art eraser and light, circular motion.

HOW TO EMBELLISH A MAT USING MARBLEIZED PAPER

MATERIALS

- Mat.
- Marbleized paper.
- Double-stick transfer tape or ATG tape.
- Hard-lead, sharp pencil.
- Mat knife.
- Metal straightedge.
- Artist's burnisher; tracing paper.

1 Cut a piece of marbleized paper about 4" (10 cm) longer than desired length of the strips. Apply double-stick transfer tape to back of paper, butting the edges; do not remove backing strip from the tape.

2 Mark right side of the paper along short ends for the desired width and number of strips. Align straightedge with marks for first strip. Using a mat knife with sharp blade, lightly score paper; repeat two or three times to cut through the paper. Gradual cutting helps seal the raw, white edges of the paper. Repeat to cut desired number of strips.

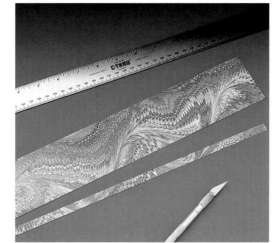

3 Mark the mat and apply paper strips as for pressure-sensitive tape, steps 1 to 5, opposite; remove paper backing from strips.

HOW TO EMBELLISH MATS USING RUB-ON TRANSFERS

MATERIALS

- Mat.
- Rub-on transfers.
- Artist's burnisher; tracing paper.

1 Remove the backing paper from transfer sheet; position the design as desired on the mat surface. Using burnisher, gently rub over design; design will lighten in color as it is released.

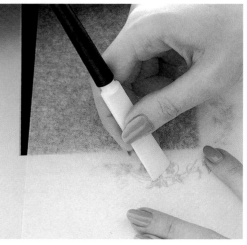

2 Lift the transfer sheet. Place backing sheet over the design; rub over design, using a burnisher.

MORE IDEAS FOR EMBELLISHED MATS

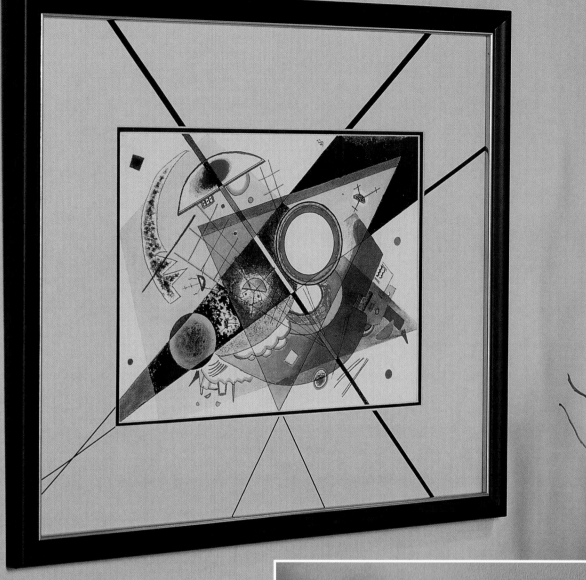

Pressure-sensitive tape (above) is used to extend the design lines in the artwork onto the mat for added drama.

Strips of paper embellish a double mat with colors found in the print.

Spattered paint (above) accents a handmade paper collage. Combine two parts paint with one part water; spatter the paint over the mat by striking the paintbrush against a paint stick.

Stamped paw-print design adds a whimsical touch to an animal print.

DISPLAYING PICTURES
IN SHIRRED FABRIC MATS

Aged prints take on an elegant, Old World look when displayed in shirred fabric mats. This easy-to-make mat is made using double-stick framer's tape and does not require any sewing. The shirred mat may be used alone, or, to create a layered double mat with a shirred inner border, it may be used under a bevel-cut mat.

To make the shirred mat, wrap the fabric around a mat cut from mat board, gathering it in your hands as it is wrapped. The mat board can be easily cut to size, using a utility knife and a straightedge.

For best results, select a lightweight fabric, such as a silk shantung or handkerchief linen. The fabric strips can be cut on either the lengthwise or crosswise grain; however, on many fabrics, it is preferable to cut the strips on the lengthwise grain, for more controlled gathers. Before cutting, you may want to gather the fabric by hand to determine the best look for the fabric you have selected.

To prevent the glass from crushing the shirred fabric, spacers are used to lift the glass from the surface of the mat. Plastic spacers with a channel designed to fit over the edge of the glass are available from framing stores. For a layered mat with an inner shirred mat, spacers are not used, because the outer mat provides the necessary space between the glass and the shirred fabric border.

When using a shirred mat with prints that you want to preserve, such as those with monetary or sentimental value, refer to the information on conservation framing on page 20. To minimize the use of acidic materials, use an acid-free mat board and acid-neutral double-stick transfer tape, or ATG tape. Also select a fabric of 100 percent natural fiber, such as silk, cotton, or linen.

Shirred fabric mats *may be used alone, as shown above, or with a bevel-cut outer mat, opposite.*

45

HOW TO MAKE A SHIRRED FABRIC MAT
& ASSEMBLE THE FRAMED PICTURE

MATERIALS

- Lightweight fabric.
- Mat board; mounting board.
- Utility knife.

- Cork-backed metal straightedge.
- Double-stick transfer tape, or ATG tape.

- Materials listed on pages 11 and 19, for mounting and assembly.
- Plastic spacers.

1 Determine size to cut mat board by subtracting ¼" (6 mm) from the dimensions of the frame opening; mark wrong side of the mat board, making sure the corners are square. Using utility knife and straightedge, score mat board along marked line; repeat until board is cut through.

2 Mark the width of mat borders, measuring from each side; image opening should be at least ⅛" (3 mm) smaller than the picture. Cut the image opening in mat board.

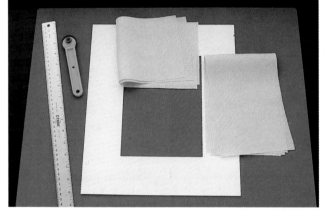

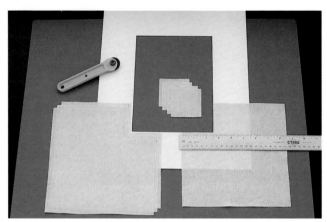

3 Cut a fabric strip for each side of the mat, with width of the strip equal to twice the width of the mat border; the length of the strip is equal to twice the length of the image opening.

4 Cut fabric squares for corner pieces, twice the width of mat border plus 2½" (6.5 cm); cut and discard 2½" (6.5 cm) squares from inner corners, to make L-shaped pieces as shown. Grainline should run in same direction on all corner pieces.

5 Place mat board facedown on table. Apply double-stick transfer tape to back of the mat board, along edges; remove paper backing.

6 Center a corner piece of fabric under the corner of the mat board. Wrap and secure the outer corner of the fabric to the corner of the mat. Wrap and secure the inner corner, creating gathers.

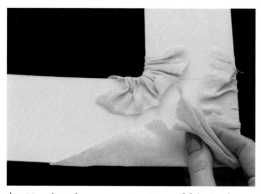

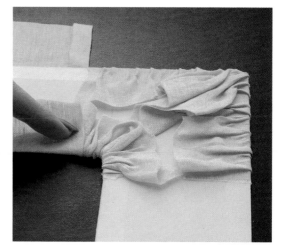

7 Hand-gather a corner piece of fabric along the inner edges; secure to the tape. Repeat along outer edges. Check appearance from right side; reposition as necessary.

8 Repeat steps 6 and 7 at the remaining corners. Fold under ½" (1.3 cm) along one short end of fabric strip for lower edge; wrap around mat, ½" (1.3 cm) from inner corner, and secure with strip of double-stick transfer tape.

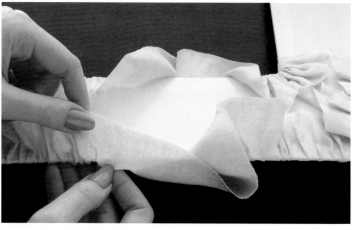

9 Hand-gather the fabric strip, and secure to tape along edges of mat board, working in sections. Fold under end of strip at opposite corner; secure with tape. Fabric may be repositioned on the tape as necessary for even distribution. Apply fabric strips to remaining sides of mat.

10 Hinge-mount the picture (pages 11 and 12). Assemble the picture in the frame (page 19); use spacers as for assembly without a mat (page 21).

HOW TO MAKE A LAYERED MAT WITH A SHIRRED INNER MAT & ASSEMBLE THE FRAMED PICTURE

1 Make the shirred inner mat as in steps 1 to 9, opposite. From mat board, bevel-cut outer mat (page 9); cut the border ½" (1.3 cm) narrower than the shirred inner mat.

2 Hinge-mount picture (pages 11 and 12), using shirred inner mat as guide for cutting the mounting board in step 5.

3 Place the outer mat faceup over the shirred inner mat. Assemble the picture in frame (pages 18 and 19); spacers are not used.

Display
Basics

DESIGN BASICS

Whether you are displaying flat artwork or three-dimensional items, following some basic design guidelines for unity, balance, proportion, color, and pattern will help you display artwork successfully.

Select artwork and accessories that reflect the mood of the room. Botanical prints emphasize the floral charm of traditional English country, while bold graphic prints complement the dramatic and streamlined styling of a contemporary decor.

When selecting the location for a wall grouping, consider the direction from which the grouping will be viewed, as well as any focal points in the room. Areas above large pieces of furniture, such as sofas, buffets, and beds, are natural choices for wall displays. Take into account how furniture and other objects positioned against a wall become part of the wall grouping. Also consider hanging artwork on the wall spaces opposite entryways. Hallways are ideal for displaying small, detailed art pieces, which are best viewed up close. Large pictures require more space for

Symmetrical arrangements have elements that are positioned identically on each side of the arrangement. Right, small shelves display statues on each side of a mirror. Above, sconces highlight a pair of companion prints.

viewing; therefore, they are best displayed where they can be viewed from a distance.

Hang artwork at eye level, taking into account whether it will be viewed from a standing or sitting position. In general, the space between a piece of furniture and a framed piece of artwork should not be more than 4" to 7" (10 to 18 cm). When hanging shelves and baskets or other dimensional items, be sure they are positioned high enough so no one will bump into them.

BALANCE

Wall arrangements can be displayed either symmetrically or asymmetrically. Symmetrical arrangements are identical on either side from the center of the display. This type of arrangement is used for a formal, traditional look. Asymmetrical groupings, when divided down the center, have two halves that look different; however, the grouping is balanced, because the visual weight on both sides is the same.

Asymmetrical arrangements have elements that are arranged differently on each side of the display. Left, shelves with decorative vases are grouped with a plate on one side of a tapestry. Above, pictures in various sizes are combined with wood medallions and a mirror.

51

Large, single rectangular picture *is in proportion to the furniture below it.*

PROPORTION

For proper proportion, the size of a wall grouping should relate in size to its surroundings. Generally, it is best to place a large display in a large space and a small display in a small space. A large display may consist of a single large item, such as a print, rug, or quilt, or it may consist of a grouping of several small items.

Unless a picture or grouping is very large, it usually needs a piece of furniture to *anchor* it, or give it a sense of belonging. In general, wall displays should not extend beyond the boundaries of the furniture positioned against the wall below.

To make a small print or picture correctly proportioned for a large space, frame it with a wide multiple mat or a wide frame molding to increase its size. In contrast, a large print can be visually reduced in size by using a narrow frame molding with a mat that blends with the wall color.

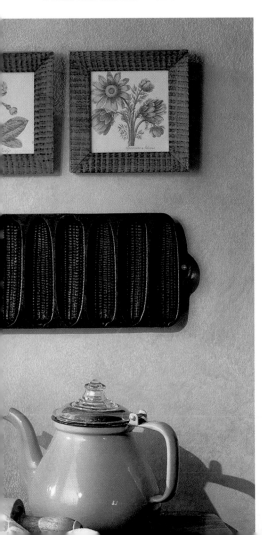

Picture and plant displayed above a chair are in proportion to the width of the chair back.

Kitchen utensils and baking pieces (opposite) are grouped with pictures to make a display that is in proportion to the side table below.

COLOR

Bold wall grouping *is created by displaying artwork that repeats the colors found in the accessories.*

When selecting artwork for wall groupings, consider the colors in the room, including the colors of the walls, fabrics, and carpet. Dark, heavy pictures and accessories placed on light-colored walls will often appear spotty. Dark-colored walls are generally easier to work with and can have light or dark groupings. For soft, subtle wall displays, choose colors that are harmonious to the room. For bolder displays, incorporate accent colors into wall arrangements. Bold colors in wall displays, that repeat the colors of accessories, such as rugs or pillows, create visual movement and a livelier atmosphere.

When framing artwork, also consider the effect the colors have on the style and the visual size of the picture. Pictures in high-contrast mats or frames appear visually larger than artwork framed for low contrast.

Colors of mats and frames *influence the style and visual size of the picture. Near right, the warm gold mat tones and frame lend a traditional look to the picture. In the center photo, the deep red mat and black frame draw the eye into the picture, visually reducing its size. On the far right, the picture takes on a contemporary look, with a neutral mat and a sleek metal frame. The lighter mat and frame visually increase the size of the picture.*

Subtle, harmonious wall grouping repeats the colors of the furnishings.

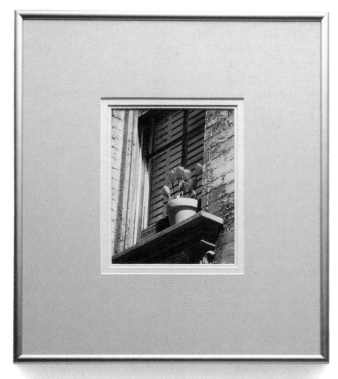

UNITY

Grouping miscellaneous pieces of artwork together requires careful consideration in order for the pieces to appear as though they belong together. Unrelated pieces can be unified by similarity of mat and frame style, color, subject matter, size of artwork, and artist's medium.

Different-size photos (above) are unified in a display of three identical-size frames by varying the size of the image openings.

Grouping of botanical prints (opposite) is a unified display because of the similarity of the subject matter, even though the mat and frame styles vary.

Collection of sports memorabilia is displayed together to create a unified grouping.

PICTURE GROUPINGS

Experiment with the placement of items in a grouping, using paper patterns. Temporarily secure paper patterns to the wall using removable tape or poster putty. Mark the placement positions lightly with a pencil.

Groupings of pictures provide visual interest and can be used to fill large wall spaces or to call attention to a unique space. Small pictures will have more impact displayed together than if displayed separately around the room.

For unique wall displays, combine accessories with a variety of shapes and textures. Plates can add both color and depth. Wall shelves can be used to display sculptures and other collectibles. Items such as bellpulls, baskets, and rugs provide additional interest.

The wall display should be contained within the dimensions of the furniture below it. Arrange items so as a group they form a shape such as a rectangle, oval, or triangle. This helps give the grouping a unified appearance.

In general, position large pictures low, and group similar sizes and shapes together. Pay attention to the spacing between pieces; if the space is too narrow, the pictures will lose their individuality. If there is too much space between the pieces of artwork, the grouping will not appear cohesive.

Before hanging a grouping, experiment by arranging the pieces on the floor until the display is pleasing to the eye. To get the proper visual perspective, make paper patterns and tape them to the wall.

TIPS FOR PICTURE GROUPINGS

Arrange frames and dimensional items so there is at least one strong vertical line or one strong horizontal line in the grouping.

Position light and dark artwork so it is balanced throughout the grouping.

Place a straight-lined piece at each end of the grouping; keep shaped items toward the center.

Use groupings of small pictures to help balance a large picture.

Position the grouping so the midpoint is at eye level.

Use vertical arrangements to emphasize or add visual height to a room; use horizontal arrangements to emphasize or add visual width to a room.

Rectangular grouping
combines several pieces of
square and rectangular
artwork.

Triangular grouping is
achieved by arranging
framed needlework in a
stair-step manner.

Oval grouping incorporates
oval and diamond shapes to
help create the silhouette.

HANGING ARTWORK

A variety of methods can be used for hanging artwork, depending on whether you are hanging framed artwork or three-dimensional items. As a precaution, when hanging heavy objects, secure the mounting hardware into a wall stud.

HOW TO HANG A PICTURE

MATERIALS

- Metal tape measure.
- Pencil.
- Picture hanger, in appropriate size for weight of picture; nail.
- Hammer.
- Carpenter's level.

1 Small or lightweight picture. Determine placement of the picture; mark the wall at the center of the top of the frame.

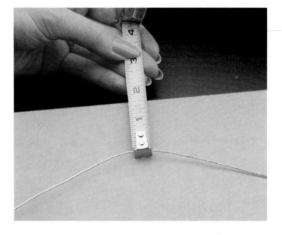

2 Pull the picture wire on the back of the frame taut, using a metal tape measure; record distance from the wire to the top of the frame.

3 Measure down from mark on wall the distance determined in step 2; mark an X. Position picture hanger so bottom of the hanger is at the X; secure with a nail.

4 Hang picture; straighten, using a carpenter's level.

1 Large or heavy picture. Follow steps 1 and 2 above, pulling the wire taut with two picture hangers as shown. Record half the distance between picture hangers. Mark an X as in step 3. Measure from the X the distance just recorded, to mark placement for a hanger on each side of X. Complete as in steps 3 and 4.

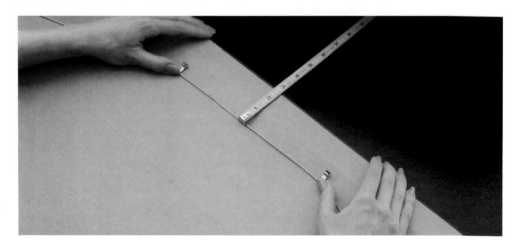